IMAGES
of Wales

ROYAL WELCH
FUSILIERS

A group of officers and men, including the Drum Major (extreme left), at Raglan Barracks, Devonport, 1899. The various types of home service uniform in use at the time can be clearly seen, as can the differences between the tall fur cap worn by officers (fourth from the right) and the shorter version worn by other ranks (first right).

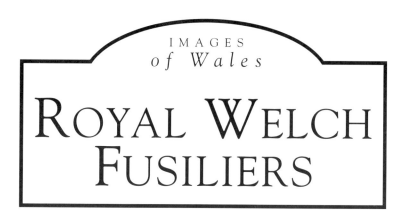

IMAGES
of Wales

ROYAL WELCH FUSILIERS

Compiled by
Peter Crocker and David Bownes
for The Royal Welch Fusiliers Museum

TEMPUS

First published 2000
Copyright © Royal Welch Fusiliers Museum, 2000

Tempus Publishing Limited
The Mill, Brimscombe Port,
Stroud, Gloucestershire, GL5 2QG

ISBN 0 7524 2061 5

Typesetting and origination by
Tempus Publishing Limited
Printed in Great Britain by
Midway Clark Printing, Wiltshire

A 'square' at the barracks at Wrexham, toward the end of the nineteenth century. It served as the Regimental Depot from 1877 to 1960. The keep is on the right. A square was the normal defence formation until the end of the nineteenth century.

Contents

A detachment of the 2nd Battalion sent from Woolwich to Windsor to perform public duties in 1871. Seated centre is Maj. T.B. Hackett wearing the Victoria Cross he won in the Indian Mutiny.

Introduction

The Royal Welch Fusiliers is Wales' oldest infantry regiment. It was raised by Lord Herbert of Chirbury at Ludlow in 1689 on the command of William III. In the following year Herbert's Regiment saw its first action at the battle of the Boyne, where the King drove the deposed James II from Ireland. The Regiment was then sent to the Low Countries where it earned its first Battle Honour at the siege of Namur in 1695.

The Regiment earned further distinctions in the War of the Spanish Succession against France. In 1702 it was one of three infantry regiments selected to be 'Fusilier' regiments whose task was to protect the artillery. This role was short-lived but it retained its honorific title. For its disciplined gallantry at the great battles of Blenheim, Ramillies, Oudenarde and Malplaquet it was styled The Royal Regiment of Welch Fusiliers.

It returned to Europe for the War of the Austrian Succession, taking part in the battles of Dettingen (1743) and Fontenoy (1745). The first recorded instance of the Regiment being called the Royal Welch Fusiliers occurred in 1727, and in 1751 it was given the number '23' when regimental order of precedence was first laid down.

The 23rd was in action again during the Seven Years War with France (1756-63). At the battle of Minden (1759) the Royal Welch was one of six British infantry regiments which destroyed the pride of the French cavalry. The 23rd also fought with distinction in the American War of Independence, most notably at Bunker Hill, Guildford Court House and Yorktown.

During the wars with Revolutionary and Napoleonic France the 23rd campaigned in the West Indies, the Low Countries, Egypt, Copenhagen, Portugal, Spain and France. A 2nd Battalion, raised in 1804, endured the appalling retreat to Corunna after the collapse of the Spanish army in 1809, and went on to participate in the ill-fated Walcheren expedition. After taking part in the battle of Copenhagen, the 1st Battalion was engaged in the capture of Martinique (1809).

In the following year it landed in the Peninsula and added further to its reputation by its disciplined courage at the battles of Albuera and Salamanca, and at the siege of Badajoz. The Regiment was also present at the battle of Waterloo (1815) where it assisted in the final rout of the French Imperial Guard and the defeat of Napoleon.

The nineteenth century saw the advent of imperial soldiering as half the British army was deployed abroad to protect the Empire. A conflict involving the European Powers was avoided until 1854 when Britain and France took the side of Turkey against Russia and war broke out in the Crimea. The 23rd fought at the battles of the Alma and Inkerman and took part in the final assault on the Redan at Sevastopol (1855). Four members of the Regiment were awarded the Victoria Cross for their gallantry during the campaign.

After a short respite in England, the 23rd was sent to India in response to the mutiny among native troops in 1857. It was present at the relief of Lucknow, where two members of the Regiment won VCs. A long period of service in India followed.

In 1873 the 2nd Battalion accompanied the expedition to Ashanti in West Africa to free prisoners held in the capital Kumassi. Soon after their return home, the 1st Battalion went to India again and while there participated in an expedition to Burma, and later joined the Hazara Black Mountain expedition on the North West Frontier (1891).

In 1881 the number '23' was omitted from the Regimental title. At about this time the old spelling of Welch was altered to Welsh, only to be officially reinstated in 1920.

During the Second Boer War (1899-1902) the 1st Battalion was engaged in several major battles, including the Relief of Ladysmith. Meanwhile, the 2nd Battalion earned a unique Battle Honour in China (1900) where it was the only British infantry unit to form part of an international force sent to suppress the Boxer rebellion.

At the outbreak of the First World War (1914-18) the Regiment had two regular battalions, a special reserve battalion, and four territorial battalions. By 1918 a total of forty-two Royal Welch battalions had served at home or overseas. The 2nd Battalion was the first to be engaged at the Retreat from Mons in August 1914, while the 4th (Denbighshire) was the first Territorial Force Battalion to reach France in December 1914. As the war progressed, Royal Welch battalions saw active service in France and Flanders, Gallipoli, Mesopotamia, Egypt, Palestine, Macedonia and Italy. The Regiment earned eighty-eight Battle Honours and over 2,800 gallantry awards. In all, 9,971 officers and men from the Regiment gave their lives during the First World War.

The twenty years which separated the First and Second World Wars saw the 1st Battalion in India, Aden and the UK. The 2nd Battalion served in Ireland, in the British Army of the Rhine in Germany (BAOR), Gibraltar, Hong Kong, Shanghai and India.

On the outbreak of the Second World War, the 1st Battalion was sent with the British Expeditionary Force to France. When the Germans invaded in May 1940 the Battalion took part in a number of delaying actions on the La Bassée Canal which helped to make the evacuation at Dunkirk possible, but only a handful of the Battalion returned home. After it was reformed in England, the Battalion went to India and later fought against the Japanese in Burma. The 2nd Battalion took part in the capture of Madagascar from the Vichy French in 1942 and then joined the 1st Battalion in Burma. The 4th, 6th and 7th Battalions landed in Normandy in June 1944 and suffered heavy casualties at Evrecy, 's-Hertogenbosch and in the Reichswald before ending the war near Hamburg.

After the war, the 2nd Battalion served as part of the army of occupation in Japan. It was disbanded, but reformed at the time of the Korean War. It served in BAOR before going to Malaya (1957-58) where it helped to defeat the Chinese communist terrorists. On return to the UK it was placed in suspended animation. Meanwhile the 1st Battalion served in Germany, the West Indies and Cyprus.

Since 1960 the 1st Battalion has spent most of its time divided between the UK, BAOR and Northern Ireland. From 1969 to 1972 it was in Hong Kong where tension with its Chinese neighbours was high. During the civil war in Yugoslavia the Battalion spent six months in Bosnia in 1995. They escorted many relief convoys through enemy held territory and during one of these Col.-Sgt Humphreys gained only the second Conspicuous Gallantry Cross to be awarded.

At the beginning of the twenty-first century, the Regiment is still very much alive and ready to face the challenges of a new era.

David Bownes and Peter Crocker

Acknowledgements

The compilers would like to thank the Trustees of the Royal Welch Fusiliers Museum for permission to publish photographs from the Museum archive, and also the Imperial War Museum for permission to reproduce those photographs indicated (IWM) in the text.

One
1689-1881

Royal Welch officers at Jubbulpore, India, in 1863. Seated in the centre is Lt-Col. Samuel Wells CB who commanded the 1st Battalion during the Indian Mutiny. He was Mentioned in Despatches three times and decorated with the CB. He retired as a Lieutenant General in 1877.

An interpretation of uniform worn by the Royal Welch Fusiliers in 1715, 1745 and 1814, by Richard Simkin, c. 1890. The very first uniform worn by the regiment was blue. After becoming a fusilier regiment in 1702, the uniform changed to the familiar red with blue facings.

An early illustration of a Royal Welch Fusilier, showing the uniform worn in 1742. The distinctive 'mitre cap' was a distinguishing feature of grenadier companies and fusilier regiments.

'Copy of a painting of Major England, Royal Welsh Fusiliers, 1828, afterward General Sir Richard England GCB', by Capt. A.R. Hutchinson, 2 RWF, Aldershot, 1874.

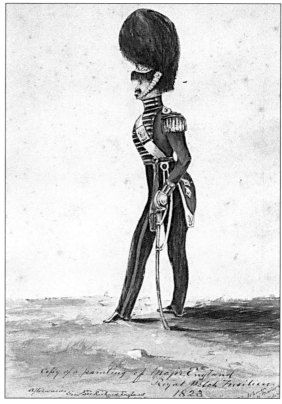

'Sacred to the Memory of Jenny Jones. Born 1789. Died at Tal-y-Llyn [North Wales] April 11th 1886. She was with her husband of the 23rd Royal Welsh Fusiliers at the Battle of Waterloo and was on the field three days.'

The Goat and Guard of Honour for Queen Victoria's visit to Bangor to open the Britannia Bridge across the Menai Straits in October 1852. This was published in the *Illustrated London News* on 23 October 1852.

The Royal Welch Fusiliers cemetery in the Crimea. Between July 1854 and September 1855, 224 died in battle and 530 of diseases.

Captain Charles Elgee (fourth from right) with a group of officers outside the Auberge de Castile in Valletta, Malta, c. 1856/57. Elgee fought with the 47th Regiment during the Crimean War. He was stationed in Malta from August 1856 until June 1857, where he fell seriously ill with a fever and spent nine weeks convalescing in this building. Elgee later commanded both the 1st and 2nd Battalions, RWF, retiring in 1885 with the rank of Major General.

A veteran of the Crimea, photographed at Landport, near Portsmouth, in 1857. The four chevrons surmounted by a crown, worn on each arm, indicate that he is a Sergeant Major. He is also wearing the British and Turkish issue Crimea medals with the French Legion of Honour. The Regiment returned from the Crimea in 1856. In February 1857 it sailed from Portsmouth for service in China, but was diverted en route and sent to India in response to the mutiny among native troops.

Pte George Monger VC. Born at Basingstoke in 1840, he enlisted in the Regiment in 1855. He was awarded the Victoria Cross for volunteering to accompany Lt Hackett in bringing in a wounded corporal under very heavy fire at Lucknow in 1857.

Officers in Lucknow, India, in 1858. On the left is Lt James Williamson RWF who had been severely wounded in the Crimea. He went on to command 2 RWF from 1885 to 1887. The other officers were in the Madras and Bengal Fusiliers, part of the East India Company's army.

An informal group of officers of the 1st Battalion in India during the 1860s. A seated officer in the front row is wearing a turban, while the officer standing third from the left wears similarly unconventional headdress.

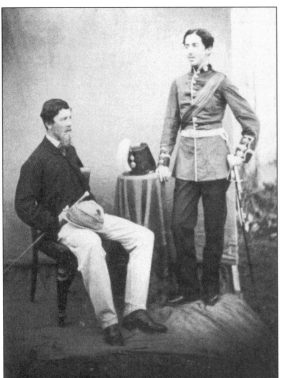

Captain the Honourable Savage Lord Mostyn (seated) with Lt Robert Bacon, 1863. Mostyn served with the Royal Welch throughout the Crimea War and Indian Mutiny. He later commanded the 2nd Battalion during the Ashanti War (1873) and was Mentioned in Dispatches three times.

Officers of the First Battalion in India, c. 1865. The Battalion was sent to India in 1857 to help suppress the Indian Mutiny and remained until 1869.

Officers of the Regimental Depot at Walmer, Kent, in 1868. This fine study illustrates the new 'quilted' style of shako introduced in 1861.

Lt E.M. Roe RWF, at the Royal
Military College, Sandhurst, 1868.

Sergeants of the RWF, c. 1870. They are wearing the early round forage cap (or 'pork pie' hat) with large numerals '23'. In the open doorway can be seen the Regimental Colours.

Ensign Charles Mayhew, 1870. He retired from the RWF in 1885 as a Major, and later became Brigade Major of the Sherwood Foresters Volunteer Infantry Brigade.

Capt. G.B. Luxford 'with a few of the articles recommended in the papers to be taken by the 2nd Batt RWF on the Ashanti Expedition, 1873-4'.

A shop in Portsmouth decorated for the return of the 2nd Battalion from the Ashanti Expedition in 1874. They were given an enthusiastic reception and presented with a goat which 'lived with the battalion for many years … on most amicable terms with his royal brother'.

An illustration of the Czar of Russia at Aldershot in May 1874 saluting the remains of the 1st Battalion Colours, which had been carried in the Crimean War. The sketch is by Lt E.H. Clough-Taylor, who carried one of the colours.

The Czar saluting the Crimean Colours of the Royal Welch Fusiliers. Aldershot 1874.

Col.-Sgt Campbell, 1 RWF, *c.* 1875. Rank was indicated by crossed flags above three chevrons, worn on the arm.

Lt Charles Ernest Clough, 2 RWF, Gibraltar, 1875. The 2nd Battalion staged in Gibraltar in October 1874 en route home from the Ashanti campaign (1873-74).

Goat Major Grey Goose of the 1st Battalion, c. 1875. The regimental tradition of wearing a leek in the hat on St David's Day can be clearly seen. This style of cap, known as the Glengarry, was introduced in 1872. It remained in use until 1890.

A group of regimental cooks, c. 1875. The man on the extreme left appears to be sharpening a knife, while two of the seated figures are enjoying a glass of beer!

Lt-Col. Luke O'Connor VC, *c.* 1879. Sergeant O'Connor won the Victoria Cross at the Battle of the Alma in 1854 for recovering the Queen's Colour and, despite being severely wounded, planting it on the Russian Redoubt. For this act of gallantry he was also commissioned as a Lieutenant and later commanded the Second Battalion. He retired on 2 March 1887 with the honorary rank of Major General, and in 1914 became Colonel of the Regiment.

Sgt (Master Tailor) Godwin and his assistants, 1 RWF, India, *c.* 1880. Each regiment at that time had a Master Tailor. A variety of uniforms can be seen undergoing repair, including a scarlet tunic and a white foreign-service jacket. Also of interest are the large flat irons, heated by filling the body of the iron with hot stones.

The Prince of Wales (later Edward VII) presenting new Colours to the 1st Battalion at Portsmouth in 1880. Col. Elgee (commanding officer) can be seen in the centre of the photograph with Maj. Tilly, carrying the Queen's Colour (left), and Maj. J Williamson carrying the Regimental Colour.

The troopship *Malabar* on which the 1st Battalion sailed for India from Portsmouth in 1880. During the voyage three men died from 'heat apoplexy' in the Red Sea.

Two

1881-1914

2 RWF on parade at Pembroke Dock, St David's Day, 1881. The Battalion's strength at this time was reported to be 13 officers, 41 sergeants and 418 privates.

Lt-Col. John Tilly, *c.* 1880. He is wearing the patrol jacket with miniature Indian Mutiny medal, and the newly introduced stiffened forage cap, which remained in use until the end of the nineteenth century. Tilly commanded 1 RWF during the campaign in Burma (1885-87).

'H' Company 1 RWF cricket team, in India, *c.* 1881.

Officers of the Denbighshire Hussars, *c.* 1890. This yeomanry regiment became the 24th Battalion, The Royal Welch Fusiliers, in March 1917. Left to right: Lt S. Platt, Lt F.E. Cotton, Capt. T. Bate, Capt. W.H. Buddicom, Capt. H.R.L. Howard, Lt-Col. A. Mesham, Dr W. Jones MD, Lt G. Blezard, Capt. O. Ormrod, Capt. S.L. Parry, Lt H.W. Buddicom, Lt O.J. Williams.

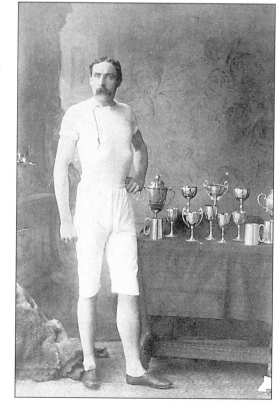

Capt. R.B. Mainwaring 'The Boxer', *c.* 1882. His trophies were won while serving with the 1st Battalion in India. He became a Brigadier during the First World War. The boxing tradition continues to the present day (see pp. 67 and 127).

Officers of the 2nd Battalion at the Curragh Camp, Ireland, in 1890. The Battalion was stationed in Ireland from 1883 to 1892.

The 2nd Battalion being welcomed by the Mayor of Caernarfon in the Square in 1892. Elements of the 4th Battalion (Royal Carnarvon and Merioneth Militia) and the 2nd Volunteer Battalion were also present.

The 2nd Battalion at Harlech Castle. In September 1892 they arrived at Holyhead, Anglesey, from Ireland where the Battalion had been stationed since 1883. It marched most of the way through North Wales to the Depot at Wrexham in order to raise recruits, camping *en route* on the estates of the local gentry.

RSM J. Henscoe (seated left) of Porthmadog and Colour Sergeants of the 2nd Volunteer Battalion, 1893. The medals indicate that it is a group of Permanent Staff Instructors from the Regular Army. The battalion was formerly the 1st Flintshire Rifle Volunteer Corps.

A signaller of the 2nd Volunteer Battalion, 1893. The principal signalling equipment consisted of flags, oil lamp (for sending messages at night) and the heliograph (depicted in the foreground). The latter consisted of a mirror mounted on a tripod by which sunlight could be flashed directly at a required point. It was used for transmitting messages in Morse code and ranges of up to seventy miles were achieved.

Drum Major J. Kensett, 1 RWF, 1894. Kensett later served with the 4th, 3rd VB, and 6th Battalions. In 1914 he was promoted Regimental Sergeant Major and helped form the 2/6th Battalion at Northampton. He was commissioned in 1917, and became Adjutant of a Prisoner of War camp in the Isle of Man.

A cartoon of Captain the Honourable Robert White. He participated in Dr Jameson's invasion of Transvaal in 1895 which led directly to the Second Boer War. He was one of eight officers convicted for their part in the raid although he was allowed to retire. He was later reinstated and went on to serve with distinction in the Boer War and the First World War.

2 RWF on parade outside the Governor's Palace, Malta, 1897. The headdress is the foreign service helmet with chinscales and spike.

Lt-Col. J.S. Roberts, Commanding Officer of the 2nd Volunteer Battalion, c. 1897. His rank is indicated by the star and crown on the shoulder cord and by the lace on the cuff.

Ceremonial Pioneers, Regimental Goat and Goat Major at Malta, 1897. The Pioneers have the white buckskin apron and gloves that has been unique to the Regiment since it was officially authorized by the Duke of Cambridge in 1886. They are also carrying their traditional axes, shovels, pick axes and mattock, a relic of the days when they prepared the way for the Regiment on the march and cleared camp sites.

Ready for kit inspection – the uniform and accoutrements of Privates Newport and Harmer, 1 RWF, laid out at Raglan Barracks, Devonport, in 1898. Above the beds can be seen the pattern 1888 valise, or 'Slade-Wallace', equipment and the full dress fur caps hanging in travelling bags. On each bed is a field service cap, hold-all (containing repair kit, cleaning and eating utensils), clothes brushes, gaiters, boots, mess tin, 'soldier's small book' (used to record service details and pay), boot polish and brushes, soap, pipe clay (for whitening valise equipment) and gloves. At the head of each bed is a haversack, towel and rifle.

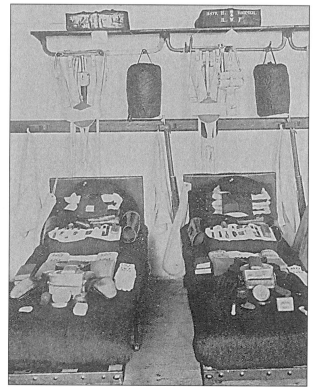

An unidentified volunteer detachment departing from Mold railway station for service in South Africa, *c.* 1901.

A RWF observation post with maxim machine gun team, South Africa, *c.* 1900. During the South African War the 1st Battalion saw action in a series of bloody battles, including Horse Shoe Hill and the Relief of Ladysmith. After this, their main job was to protect the army supply lines from guerilla attack.

Officers of the 2nd Volunteer Active Service Company, prior to embarkation for South Africa, c. 1900-01. By this stage in the war, many regiments had abandoned the foreign service helmet in favour of the slouch hat depicted here, which was better suited for conditions in the Transvaal. Left to right: Lt W.M. Griffith (1st VB RWF), Capt. H. Meredith-Jones (1st VB RWF), Lt R.T. Ford (2nd VB RWF).

Battle hardened veterans of the 1st Battalion, South Africa, 1902. The gruelling experiences of the South African War are written onto the faces of the soldiers depicted here, many of whom would have been on active service for several years. The uniforms also show the effects of war. Only the cloth badge on the Foreign Service helmet indicates that they are Royal Welch Fusiliers.

Cyclists of the 2nd Volunteer Battalion in camp at Fleetwood, 1900. Bicycles were first introduced to the British Army during the 1880s. Companies of cyclists, like this one, were a common feature of volunteer battalions, where they were trained as messengers and dispatch riders.

Sergeants and buglers of the 4th Battalion (Royal Carnarvon and Merioneth Militia) in 1900 at the Barracks, Caernarfon, which was built for the Militia in 1855. The Battalion was disbanded in 1908 as part of army reforms.

The Band of the 2nd Volunteer Battalion in camp at Conwy, 1901. The regimental band was once a distinctive feature of British infantry. The traditional marching music of the RWF remains the *British Grenadiers* and *Men of Harlech*.

An RWF Maxim machine-gun team at the beginning of the twentieth century. The Maxim gun, seen here on its wheeled carriage, was brought into general service with the British Army in 1890. Although superseded by the Vickers machine gun in 1912, it was still in use with the RWF during the early part of the First World War.

Men of the 2nd Battalion on board HMS *Terrible*, en route to Tientsin, China, June 1900. The Battalion was despatched to China from Hong Kong as part of an international force to suppress the 'Boxer' rebellion which had resulted in the massacre of foreigners in China. The Battalion was the only British one present and the Battle Honour 'Relief of Pekin' in unique to the Regiment.

The ruined engine shed at Tientsin railway station, China, where the Royal Welch Fusiliers fought alongside the United States Marine Corps in 1900 – thus beginning a close relationship which exists to this day.

Members of 2 RWF resting in the British Legation grounds, Peking, August 1900, after control of the area had been wrested from the Boxers.

Officers from the 2nd Battalion returning to Hong Kong from China on board the transport *Salamis*, October 1900. Left to right: Capt. H.O.S. Cadogan, 2nd-Lt H. Grant Smith (East Yorkshire Regiment), Capt. H.M. Richards, 2nd-Lt W.G. Vyvyan, Lt & QM J.F. Clieve, unidentified officer (Royal Engineers), Capt. Prynne (RAMC), Capt. J.H. Gwynne, Lt-Col. Hon RH Bertie, Maj. Reilly (RAMC), Capt. A. Hay, Maj. C.M. Dobell, Lt C.S. Owen, Lt O.S. Flower, Lt F.J. Walwyn, Lt R.I.B. Johnson.

'C' Company of the 2nd Battalion taking a break during training in Chakrata, India, 1904. Frank Richards, a signaller with 2 RWF in 1904 and author of *Old Soldier Sahib*, described India as 'the land of milk and honey', where peacetime soldiering and regular wages resulted in a high standard of living for many servicemen – especially when compared with the living and working conditions they had left behind in Britain.

The 2nd Battalion, led by the band, marching from Chakrata to Meerut in November 1903. They took part in hill manoeuvres on the way.

'Types of the 2nd Battalion', India, 1904. A wide variety of uniforms were in use with the Regiment at this time, ranging from the full dress scarlet tunic worn by the officer in the centre of the picture, to the apron and gauntlets of the Pioneers at either end of the group. Despite the variety on show, there are a number of orders of dress not depicted.

An outing by members of 2 RWF Sergeants' Mess and their families at Chakrata, India, in 1903.

The successful 2nd Battalion football team at Meerut, India, 1903. The Sergeant on the left is wearing the short-lived Brodrick cap (1902-05). The Company Sergeant Major, seated to the right of the cup, has the China War Medal 1900, with the clasp 'Relief of Pekin'.

Officers at breakfast in India, June 1904. From left to right: Capt. F.J. Walwyn DSO, 2nd-Lt E.C.C. Lloyd, Capt. G.F.H. Dickson, 2nd-Lt S. Jones, Capt. F.C. France-Hayhurst, 2nd-Lt J.R.M. Minshull-Ford. Their native servants are also present.

Members of a volunteer battalion band taking part in the Caernarfon Regatta, 1903. The boat is moored in front of Caernarfon Castle at the mouth of the Seiont River.

Permanent Staff Instructors of the 2nd Volunteer Battalion, in camp at Fleetwood, 1904. The embroidered crossed rifles on the right arm of the sergeants' tunics indicates that they are Instructors of Musketry. Left to right, back row: Sgt S. Bowyer, Sgt W. Jones, Sgt J. Jelly, Sgt H. Joy. Front row: Sgt F. Ruscoe, Sgt A. Whybro, Sgt-Maj. G. Claridge, Capt. & Adjt C.E. Willes, Sgt Vale, Sgt N. Ridings.

The Dining Hall of the Regimental Depot, Wrexham, *c.* 1905. The tables are laid out with crested china, usually stored in the wooden racks on the wall. According to a young recruit of the time, dinner at the Depot consisted of either a roast, stew or curry. On the command of the canteen orderly, soldiers were allowed to rush the serving plates for 'seconds' – with the result that fights were not uncommon!

The Regimental goat, *c.* 1905. The first mention of the custom that the Regiment marches with a goat with gilded horns at its head appeared in 1777 in a book which commented on 'the ancientness of the custom'. In 1844 Queen Victoria presented the first Royal Goat and since then the regular battalions and most of the territorial battalions have usually had a goat presented by the Sovereign.

Polo playing officers of the 2nd Battalion at Agra, India, *c*. 1904/5. The Battalion had over 100 polo ponies, and was able to field two teams at the same time, the 1st playing at Meerut, and the 2nd at Delhi and Cawnpore. Left to right: 2nd-Lt N.M. Wilson (on 'Clown'), Lt M.E. Lloyd (on 'Boskey'), Capt. G.F.H. Dickson (on 'Red Ensign') and 2nd-Lt E.R. Kearsley (on 'Blue Ruin').

The Prince and Princess of Wales' visit to 2 RWF at Agra, India, in 1905. The Prince had been Colonel of the Regiment since 1901. Seated between Their Royal Highnesses is the Commanding Officer, Brevet Colonel H.T. Lyle DSO, who had been awarded the decoration for his service in Burma in 1885-87 with the 1st Battalion.

Sergeants of 'H' Company, 2 RWF, about to embark on a hunting expedition in Bhamo, Burma, 1908.

F. Scovell   18, Queen's Road, Aldershot.

Pte W. Hughes 1 RWF, Aldershot, c. 1904-07. The 1st Battalion was stationed in England on its return from South Africa in 1903. *Carte de visite* photographs like this one were still popular, although it was more usual for a photograph to be reproduced as a postcard which could be sent to friends and relatives.

Officers of the 3rd Battalion (Royal Denbigh and Flint Militia) at Conwy Camp, 1906. They are wearing the high collared pattern service dress introduced in 1902. The brass letter 'M' worn beneath the grenade collar badge, indicates that they are Militia officers.

The 2nd Battalion on parade at Agra, India, 1907. Between 1896 and 1914 the Battalion was continually overseas in Malta, Crete, Egypt, Hong Kong, China, Burma and India.

A parade outside the Officers' Quarters at the Regimental Depot, *c.* 1910. The Russian cannon was captured in the Crimean War in 1854 by Capt. E.W.D. Bell who was awarded a Victoria Cross for his gallantry.

Members of 2 RWF lining the route in Delhi during the Durbar in December 1911. 'Durbar' is the Indian word for meeting. King George V and Queen Mary were meeting with the Indian Princes to receive homage to them.

Officers of the 1st and 2nd Battalions dining in Malta on St David's Day 1914. The 1st Battalion had arrived from England in January. The 2nd Battalion was en route home from India. It was the first occasion on which the two battalions had met since 1880. An officer may be seen 'eating the leek'.

Three
1914-1918

The 6th (Carnarvonshire and Anglesey) Battalion marching past Caernarfon Castle just prior to the outbreak of war. The Battalion later served in Gallipoli, Egypt and Palestine.

A picture of 1788 Pte William Lewis RWF, illustrating the uniform worn by infantry soldiers in France and Flanders. He is holding the short magazine Lee Enfield .303 rifle, which was used throughout the war.

Members of the 1/5th (Flintshire) Battalion at dinner near Northampton in August 1914, shortly after the declaration of war. The Battalion went on to serve in Gallipoli, Egypt and Palestine.

A group of regimental signallers with signalling flags. Eight of the seventeen in this picture have the name 'Jones'. To avoid confusion, Royal Welch Fusiliers are known by the last two digits of their army number, such as Jones 43 and Jones 86.

Lt (later Captain) W.J. Crutch seated on a 'New Imperial' motorcycle, *c.* 1915. Crutch was the transport officer of the 2/4th (Denbighshire) Battalion. The Battalion was formed in Wrexham in 1914 and served in England throughout the war.

Transport officer and staff of the 2/4th Battalion, at Northampton, May 1915. The men are dressed for stable duties, and several are equipped with horse brushes. The seated corporal is holding a young kid – possibly the Battalion's unofficial goat.

Transport Sergeant Thomas Arthur Humphries on the occasion of his wedding, August 1915. Humphries was a pre-war regular soldier. He served with the 1st Battalion in France, Flanders and Italy, where he was awarded the Italian War Cross. Like many pre-war members of the battalion, Humphries came from Birmingham.

Officers of the 9th Battalion in England in 1915. Shortly before their departure for France in July, the commanding officer, Lt-Col. Sir Horace McMahon DSO (seated centre) retired because of ill health and was replaced by Maj. H.J. Maddocks (seated on McMahon's right) who was killed in action in September 1915.

Lt-Col. C.H.M. Doughty-Wylie VC, CB, CMG. He joined the Regiment in 1889, and was awarded the CMG in 1904 for his services in saving lives during the Turkish massacre of Armenians. He received the CB in 1914 for work in Albania on behalf of the Foreign Office. On 26 August 1915 he organized and led an attack on a strong Turkish position at Sedd-el-Bahr, Gallipoli, and was killed at the moment of victory and posthumously awarded the Victoria Cross.

Machine gunners of the 2/6th Battalion at Bedford, c. 1915. The 2/6th was a 'second line' battalion and remained in England throughout the war. On the left is a Vickers gun, on the right a Lewis gun, and in between a range finder.

Reinforcements at Wrexham station waiting to depart for the front, *c.* 1915. The officer in the centre is Lt-Col. H.R. Jones-Williams who was the commanding officer of 3 RWF until June 1917.

Maj. A.H. Wheeler, 6 RWF. A pre-war Territorial officer, Wheeler accompanied the Battalion to Gallipoli in 1915. He landed at Suvla Bay on 9 August, and was killed advancing from the beachhead on the following day.

'Old Sweats', 2 RWF, 1915. Sgt Davies is seated at the front. The man on the right is holding the jar which contained the rum ration.

Horse drawn transport belonging to 1st Battalion, France 1915.

Bomb damaged buildings used as billets by 2 RWF, at Bois-Grenier, France, in 1915. The scene was revisited by the Battalion in March 1918 during the final German offensive. Capt. Moody, a battalion officer on both occasions, recorded that the original communication trenches were still in place, although the buildings had been reduced to heaps of rubble.

CSM Frederick Barter VC, 1 RWF. He won the VC at Festubert on 16 May 1915 after leading an attack which captured 105 German officers and men and 500 yards of enemy trenches. He was also awarded a Military Cross in Palestine in 1918.

The 3rd (Special Reserve) Battalion postman at Litherland Training Camp, 1915. The Battalion was at Litherland, near Liverpool, from 1915 to 1917 before moving to Ireland. It served as a Reserve for the Territorial as well as the Regular and New Army (or Service) battalions. By August 1918 the Battalion had trained almost 20,000 recruits, who saw active service with the RWF in all theatres of war.

Lunchtime at Litherland. Young recruits take a break during training in June 1915.

The pastry making hut at Litherland, *c.* 1916. At this time there were about 2,000 men undergoing training at Litherland Camp.

A soldier's kit laid out for inspection at Litherland Camp, *c.* 1916. Each item is marked as being the property of 3 RWF and carries the soldier's regimental number.

Capt. Macdonald and RSM Jones of the 15th (Service) Battalion (1st London Welsh). The Battalion was raised in November 1914, initially from Welshmen living in London. It served on the Western Front as part of the 38th Division (113 Brigade) and was disbanded in February 1918. (IWM)

Sgt Joseph J. Davies, VC, 10 RWF. Davies won the Victoria Cross at Delville Wood, France, on 20 July 1916, where he single-handedly repulsed a German counter-attack and extricated a group of soldiers under his command after their position had become untenable. He was one of eight Royal Welchmen to receive the award during the war.

Dog carts were used during the war to take supplies up to the front line.

Officers of the 15th (Service) Battalion (1st London Welsh). The embroidered dragon arm badge of the 38th (Welsh) Division is visible on the tunics of officers on the right of the photograph.

'C' Company of the 4th (Denbighshire) Battalion. This pre-war Territorial Force battalion was sent to France in November 1914. It became the pioneers of the 47th Division.

Officers of the 2nd Battalion at Buire on the Somme, early August 1916. In July they had fought at Albert, Bazentin Ridge and High Wood. Left to right, back row: Lt H.E.G. Goldsmith, Capt. P.S. Wilson (killed in action in August 1916), Capt. M. Williams MC, Capt. N.H. Radford, 2nd-Lt C.R.J.R. Dolling MC (killed in action in August 1916), Capt. G.F. Wolff (killed in action in 1918), Capt. A.W. Loverseed, Capt. E. Coster MC (killed in action in 1917). Middle row: Lt F.R.C. Barnett, Capt. J.C. Dunn MC, DCM, RAMC, Lt-Col. C.H.R. Crawshay, Capt. J.V. Higginson MC, Lt & QM H. Yates. Front row: Lt F.W. Jagger, 2nd-Lt A.T. Harries, 2nd-Lt E.C. Tunnicliffe, 2nd-Lt H. Robertson.

A surprisingly high number of war poets and authors served with the Royal Welch, the best known being Siegfried Sassoon and Robert Graves (top left and centre), whose works include *Memoirs of an Infantry Officer* and *Goodbye to All That*. Other writers from the Regiment included Frank Richards, *Old Soldiers Never Die* (top right), Llewelyn Wyn Griffith, *Up to Mametz* (bottom left), and Dr J.C. Dunn, *The War the Infantry Knew*. Poet and artist David Jones (bottom right), author of *In Parenthesis*, was also a Royal Welchmen, as was the Welsh bard Ellis Humphrey Evans (*Hedd Wyn*), who was killed in action in 1917. Their moving testimonies have helped shape the responses of generations to the experience of the 'Great War'.

Col.-Sgt Isaac Roberts with fellow NCOs of the 1/6th (Carnarvonshire & Anglesey) Battalion in Cairo, January 1917. The Battalion served in Gallipoli, Egypt and Palestine with the 53rd (Welsh) Division.

L/Cpl R. Williams, Goat Major, and the Regimental Goat, 2 RWF, at Cavillon in France, 18 July 1917. (IWM)

Sgt Johnny Basham. He enlisted in the Regiment in 1911. In 1914 he became the Welterweight Champion of Great Britain and was the first soldier ever to win a Lonsdale Belt. He retained the title in 1915 and 1916, winning the Belt outright. He once fought three rounds with Robert Graves. Basham served as a PT instructor in France in 1917.

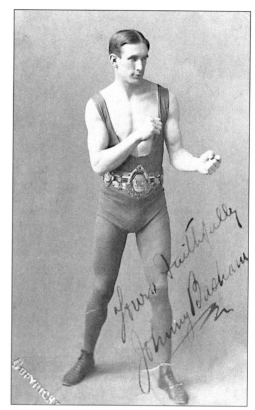

Lt J.D.M. Richards of 'C' Company 2 RWF who was wounded and missing on 27 May 1917 in operations on the Hindenburg Line. He became a prisoner of war and lost his leg.

Rememberance: a sombre Christmas message for 1917 from the Welsh Horse Yeomanry members of the 25th Battalion. The WHY was raised in August 1914 in South Wales. It served in Gallipoli before going to Egypt where, in March 1917, it amalgamated with the Montgomeryshire Yeomanry to become the 25th Battalion, RWF. After fighting in Palestine, 25 RWF was sent to France in May 1918 to help counter the German offensive.

Officer and men of the 5th/6th Battalion in Alexandria, Egypt, 1919. The Battalion was formed in August 1918 out of an amalgamation between the 5th and 6th Battalions, caused by heavy casualties. On the upper arm they wear the battalion identification badge of a black diamond with central red and white stripes.

Sgt N.C. Jones and S/Sgt Doran, 5/6 RWF in Alexandria, Egypt, 1919.

The only members of 2 RWF to serve with the Battalion from landing in France in August 1914 until returning to Britain in May 1919. Left to right: Capt. W.H. Fox MC, Armourer Sgt J. Belfield, Lt D. Roberts-Morgan DCM MM, Sgt Childs, Sgt Drummer Dyer MM. MSM, Cpl Davies, RQMS J. Hughes DCM, L/Cpl Wright, Driver Carrol, Capt. & QM H. Yates MC.

Officers of 1 RWF in St Mark's Square, Venice, December 1918. The Battalion was sent to Italy in 1917 with a British Force to reinforce the Italian Army reeling from an Austrian offensive.

An early design for the headstones of RWF graves, commissioned by the Commonwealth War Graves Commission (CWGC). The actual design chosen differed from the one depicted here in the spelling of 'Welch'. The permanent headstones erected by the CWGC in the 1920s were all of uniform pattern, showing the badge of the dead soldier's unit above a simple inscription, irrespective of rank or social status.

Four

1918-1939

Lt-Gen. Sir Francis Lloyd, Colonel of the Regiment, unveiling of the Regimental War Memorial at Wrexham on 15 November 1924. It commemorates the 9,971 Royal Welch Fusiliers who gave their lives during the First World War. It was designed by Sir William Goscombe John RA.

Officers of the 4th Battalion (TA) at Foryd Camp, Rhyl, in August 1920. Left to right, back row: 2nd-Lt A. Wynne, 2nd-Lt O.E. Roberts, Lt H.M.P. Dennis, Lt E.W. Peate MC, 2nd-Lt P.W. Brundrit, Lt A.I. Phillips, 2nd-Lt O.A. Davies, Lt L.I. Davies. Front row: Capt. T.R. Williams MC, Capt. H.W. Davies MC, Capt. P.R. Foulkes-Roberts MC, Lt-Col. J.C. Davies TD MO, Lt-Col. J.R. Minshull-Ford DSO MC, Maj. G.C.W. Westbrooke MC, Capt. & Adjt M.A. Lloyd-Mostyn, Capt. D. Seymour-Jones, Capt. J.W. McKill, Capt & QM T. Manfield.

The Corps of Drums, 1 RWF, Lucknow, India in 1920. Boys were often employed as drummers, buglers and fifers. Left to right, front row, seated: RSM Wylie, Lt & Adjt (later Maj.-Gen.) M.B. Dowse, Lt-Col. (later Brigadier) C.S. Owen, Lt B.E. Horton and the Drum Major. The others are unknown.

The parade at the Depot, Wrexham, on 9 August 1921, when Silk Union Flags were presented to the 8th, 10th, 11th, 15th and 19th Service Battalions and the 1st, 2nd and 6th Garrison Battalions, by the Colonel of the Regiment, Lt-Gen. Sir Francis Lloyd. The flags were presented in recognition of the contribution made by the Battalions in the First World War.

Maj. G.L. Compton-Smith DSO. He served with the RWF in France during the First World War and commanded 10 RWF at the first battle of the Scarpe in 1917. He received the DSO and French Legion of Honour. After the war, he served with 2 RWF in Ireland where he was taken hostage by the IRA in 1921 and later shot.

The machine-gun section of the 2nd Battalion at Phoenix Park, Dublin, 7 June 1922. The officers seated in the centre of the group are Lt (later Lt-Col.) H.C. Watkins OBE, MC and Lt J.A. Pringle MC. The soldiers in the foreground are manning Vickers machine guns. In 1919 2 RWF had been sent to Ireland to help maintain British rule.

The 2nd Battalion leaving Phoenix Park Barracks, Dublin, December 1922. Following the signing of the peace treaty in December, the British Army withdrew from Southern Ireland, thus ending a long association between the Regiment and military camps such as the Curragh and Phoenix Park, which had been the home of the Royal Welch on many occasions.

St David's Day at Tauda China, Waziristan, 1 March 1923. The 1st Battalion served on the North-West Frontier of India from December 1921 to March 1923 where they carried out operations against Mahsud tribesmen.

Split Hill Piquet, Waziristan, 1923. On 5 February six members of the Regiment were killed by tribesmen, and four were awarded Military Medals for rescuing wounded comrades under fire.

Maj. E.O. Skaife in India, *c.* 1924. Skaife, who later commanded 1 RWF (1929-33), learnt Welsh and Russian as a German prisoner during the First World War. He was Military Attaché in Moscow (1934-37) and commanded 158th (Royal Welsh) Infantry Brigade from 1937 to 1941. He became Colonel of the Regiment in 1948 and was appointed to the Druidic Order of the Gorsedd in 1956, the year in which he was knighted for public service in Wales.

The 1st Battalion boxing team, winners of the All India Boxing Tournament, 1924/25, Mussoorie, India.

The annual camp of 158th Welsh Brigade at Porthcawl, *c.* 1927/28. All the officers are members of the Regiment. Left to right, standing: Capt. H.B. Harrison MC (later CO 1 RWF, killed in action in 1940), Maj. D.M. Barchard (Brigade Major), Capt. E.R. Freeman, Capt. H.F. Garnons-Williams (later CO 1 RWF, killed in action in 1939), Lt Ll Gwydyr Jones (later CO 2 RWF), Lt W.H. Bamfield. Seated: Col. G.C.W. Westbrooke MC (CO 4 RWF), Col. C.C. Norman CMG, DSO, Lt-Gen. Sir Charles Dobell CMG, DSO (Colonel of the Regiment), Col. F. Walwyn DSO, Lt-Col. A.M. Trustram-Eve MC (CO 6 RWF and later Lord Silsoe).

1 RWF in camp at Yaru, India, 1928. The battalion served in India from 1919 to 1930.

Lieutenant Commander J.P. Sousa, the American composer, presenting the score of his march *The Royal Welch Fusiliers* to Gen. Sir Charles Dobell, Colonel of the Regiment, at Tidworth on 25 June 1930. The piece was composed to mark the close association between the United States Marine Corps and the Regiment which began in China in 1900.

Machine-gun Company, 2 RWF, Tidworth, 1930. At the rear are four D-Type Morris Commercial vehicles used as personnel carriers. The tracked vehicles are Corden-Lloyds which carried a Vickers machine gun and crew of five.

The 1st Battalion on exercise in England, 1935. The Battalion was stationed in England from 1932 until the outbreak of war in 1939.

The Red Dragon and Barnett-Barker Races, near Beaumaris, Anglesey, Friday 13 March 1936. The Red Dragon Challenge Cup was competed for by serving RWF officers riding their own horses, while the Barnett-Barker Cup was for officers riding government horses allotted to the Regiment. Both races were run simultaneously over a distance of five miles. The winners on this day were Maj. E. Wodehouse on *Benedict* and Lt H.A.S. Clarke on *Cherry Lad*.

The 4th Battalion (TA) at Wrexham general railway station, returning from camp in Harlech, *c.* 1935/36.

A group of officers of the 2nd Battalion in Shanghai, 1937. Seated, third from the right, is the Commanding Officer, Lt-Col. D.M. Barchard. The Battalion had been sent to Shanghai at very short notice to protect foreigners endangered by the Japanese advance in the opening stages of the Sino-Japanese War.

Christmas Day celebrations in the Corporal's Mess, 2 RWF, Shanghai, 1937.

King George VI inspecting the Guard of Honour provided by 1 RWF during his visit to Caernarfon, 15 July 1937. The King is accompanied by Maj. H.A. Freeman.

David Lloyd George inspecting the goats of the 1st, 4th, 6th and 7th Battalions, accompanied by the Lord Lieutenant and Major General JRM Minshull-Ford, on the occasion of the Regiment's 250th Anniversary, Caernarfon Castle, August 1939. The anniversary was celebrated with parades at Wrexham and Caernarfon. In his address to the Regiment, Lloyd George, who had been Prime Minister during the last two years of the First World War, warned against the 'menace to human liberties, which now hangs in the firmament, like a dark thundercloud.' Four weeks later war was declared on Germany.

Five

1939-1945

Prime Minister
Winston
Churchill
inspecting the
8th Battalion
Goat at Dover,
1943.

Officers of 1 RWF at Blackdown before embarking for France, September 1939. The Battalion was annihilated in May 1940 covering the British withdrawal to Dunkirk. Only 5 officers and 263 other ranks returned to England out of over 1,000. Left to right, back row: Lt C. Griffiths, Lt A.N.B. Sugden, 2nd-Lt M.J.B. Kemp, 2nd-Lt J.L. King, Lt J.E.C. Hood, Lt H.G. Brougham, 2nd-Lt W.J. Griffiths, 2nd-Lt R.S. Best, Capt. H.A.S. Clarke. Middle row: Lt W.P.D. Skillington, Lt A.B. Powell, Lt J.E.T. Willes, Capt. A.D.M. Lewis MBE, Capt. A.J. Lewis, 2nd-Lt F.M. Edwards, Capt. E.C. Parker Jervis, Lt R.F.A. David, Lt R.O.F. Prichard, Lt & QM A.G. Bent MM. Front row: Capt. L.H. Yates, Maj. R.L.K. Allen, Maj. D.I. Owen, Maj. H.D.T. Morris, Lt-Col. H.F. Garnons-Williams, Capt. W.L.R. Benyon, Maj. H.B. Harrison MC, Capt. O.T.M. Raymont, Capt. J.R. Johnson.

Tactical Exercise Without Troops (TEWT): Company Commanders from the 60th (RWF) Anti-Tank Regiment RA (TA) undergoing training in the tactical deployment of troops at Hafod-y-Coed, 1939. The Battalion was formed in 1938 from the 5th (Flints) Battalion RWF (TA). In the centre of the group are Capt. H.S.K. Mainwaring and Capt. R. Charlton.

Members of the North Wales area Local Defence Volunteers (LDV), later the 5th Battalion (Caernarvonshire) Home Guard, 1940. The Home Guard, as the LDV became in August 1940, was raised to relieve regular soldiers of certain duties within the UK. Twenty-six battalions were badged RWF. Early shortages of uniform meant that many wore civilian dress.

The 1st Battalion Goat being prepared for St David's Day duties, France, 1 March 1940. The Goat Major is painting the horns gold – an ancient practice, which was abolished after it was discovered to damage the goat's health.

St David's Day, France, 1 March 1940. A fusilier keeps watch with a Bren-gun, although at this date full-scale war with Germany was yet to break out.

1 RWF under enemy artillery fire while dug-in near the River Dyle, May 1940.

Capt. R.O.F. Prichard and men of 1 RWF digging-in on the Belgian Frontier, 1940.

'A Memory of France – the flag that accompanied the Royal Welch to France and the soldier who brought it back from Dunkirk': an insert from a regimental Christmas card, 1940. This tattered flag can be seen when it was still in pristine condition in the photograph of the Regimental Goat on St David's Day, 1940.

Cpl W. Wood of No. 1 Battalion (Denbighshire) Home Guard, demonstrates their 'most popular weapon' – the sten.

A sergeant and carrier pigeon from the 6th Battalion (Royal Welch), The Parachute Regiment. The 10th Battalion was given this title when it was selected to become a parachute battalion in 1942. It fought in Italy before parachuting into southern France in 1944. In 1945 the Battalion assisted the Greek government in its civil war with the communists.

A member of the 6th Battalion (Royal Welch), The Parachute Regiment, undergoing training. When it became a parachute battalion it uniquely preserved in its new title the name of its former regiment. The Goat, Flash and St David's Day celebrations were all retained as part of the Royal Welch tradition.

Royal Welch Fusiliers undergoing training with respirators at the Gas Chamber, Lille Barracks, Farnborough.

Bofors guns of 116 Light Anti-Aircraft Regiment, RA – formerly 12th (Home Defence) Battalion, RWF. The Regiment was formed in 1940. It fought with the 53rd (Welsh) Division as anti-aircraft gunners in north-west Europe. It was the first element of the Royal Welch Fusiliers to land in Normandy.

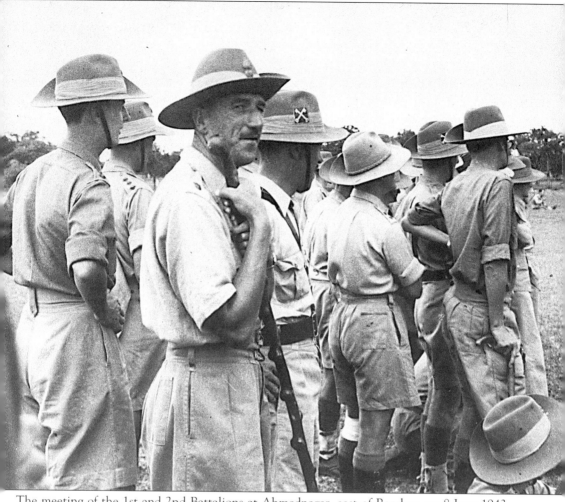

The meeting of the 1st and 2nd Battalions at Ahmednagar, east of Bombay, on 8 June 1943. Lt-Col. Ll Gwydyr-Jones, commanding 2 RWF, with his famous jungle stick, faces the camera, and alongside him, Lt-Col. A.H. Williams DSO, commanding 1 RWF.

1 RWF patrol in the Arakan, Burma, 1944. After reforming in the UK the battalion was sent to India and fought in Burma, 1943-45.

One of 2 RWF's transport mules bogged down in the mud of a Burmese jungle track, 1944. Poor roads and impenetrable jungle were some of the many difficulties experienced during the campaign against the Japanese.

Members of 2 RWF crossing the Nankye Cheung near Mawlu, Burma, November, 1944. After participating in the invasion of Madagascar, in 1942, the Battalion was sent to India and fought in Burma in 1944-45. (IWM)

A section of 2 RWF passing a 3-inch Mortar detachment during the preparations for the attack on Pinwe, Burma, November 1944.

Men of 2 RWF digging in, protected by a Bren gunner, prior to the attack on Pinwe, Burma, 30 November 1944.

Lt-Col. A.H. Williams DSO (left), commanding 1 RWF in Burma, 1944. He won the DSO at the battle of Donbaik, Burma, in 1943. Field Marshal Sir William Slim later wrote, 'It was a battle which should never have been fought … The last and final assault was led by the Royal Welch Fusiliers and on that day they showed valour which I think has rarely been surpassed'.

Unveiling of the RWF memorial at Kuki's Piquet, Kohima, in November 1944. The 1st Battalion took part in the bitter fighting to capture the Japanese stronghold at Kohima, Burma, in April 1944. Victory was only secured with high losses, against a determined and well-prepared enemy.

Lt-Col. J.A.M. Rice-Evans (centre), 4 RWF, issuing orders before the battle of Evrecy, France, 16 July 1944. This battle proved to be a bloody baptism of fire for the three Territorial battalions (4th, 6th & 7th), which suffered heavy casualties. (IWM)

A 3-inch Mortar detachment of 7 RWF during a lull in firing near Hanssum, Holland, 8 December, 1944. In six days the Mortar Platoon fired over 1,000 rounds. (IWM)

A Royal Welch Fusilier patrol on the west bank of the Maas river, 9 December 1944. (IWM)

A section of the 6th Battalion, weighed down with full equipment, waiting to advance in 1945. (IWM)

Men of the 6 RWF in the Ardennes, Belgium, January 1945. British troops had been sent to reinforce American resistance to Hitler's final offensive launched in December 1944. (IWM)

4 RWF Anti-Tank Platoon receiving orders prior to the attack on Gyhum, Germany, April 1945. (IWM)

Members of the 4th Battalion clearing a house at Host, Holland, February 1945, where seventy-two prisoners were taken.

Dr Artur Seyss-Inquart, former
Chancellor of Austria and, from 1940,
Reichskommissar for Holland, after his
capture by Fusilier William Taylor,
6 RWF, in May 1945. Seyss-Inquart
was subsequently tried at Nuremberg
for war crimes and executed.

Field Marshal Montgomery,
Commander-in-Chief British Forces of
Occupation in Germany, inspecting
members of the Regiment at
Düsseldorf, 1945.

Six

1945-2000

Her Majesty The Queen, Colonel-in-Chief, with the Colonel of the Regiment, Lt-Gen. Sir Hugh Stockwell, on the occasion of the Presentation of Colours to the 1st, 2nd and 4th (TA) Battalions, at Wroughton, 23 July 1954.

Gen. Sir Claude Auchinleck inspecting 2 RWF prior to their leaving India for Japan, 15 January 1946. The General is talking to Sgt Plimmer. Behind him are Lt-Col. M.H. ap Rhys Pryce and Capt. Hill.

The Pioneers and Drums of 2 RWF on parade, Japan 1946. At the end of the war the 2nd Battalion went to Japan as part of the army of occupation, returning to Britain in 1948.

A representative party from the 2nd Battalion with King George VI at Buckingham Palace on the occasion of the disbandment of the battalion, 15 July 1948. Left to right, back row: Fus Adams, Sgt Bull, RQMS Brant, Sgt Lewis, RSM Evans, Sgt Ridings, Cpl Percival, Capt. A.R.R. Davies. Front row: Capt. & QM J. Brown, Lt-Col. Ll Gwydyr-Jones, Lt-Gen. Sir Charles Dobell, Brig E.O. Skaife, King George VI, Lt-Col. J.A.M. Rice-Evans, Maj.-Gen. H.C. Stockwell, Maj. R. Snead-Cox, Maj. J.D. Willans.

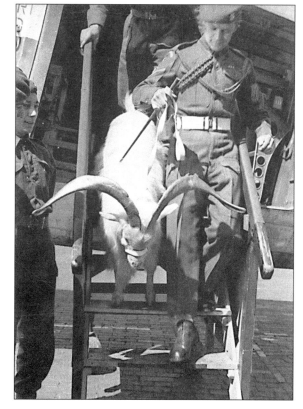

The Regimental Goat of the 1st Battalion arriving in Berlin, 14 April 1949. The Battalion assisted the airlift of food and supplies for the Berlin people trapped by the year long Russian blockade. Forty years later, the battalion was again in Berlin, when the 'fall' of the Berlin Wall led to the reunification of Germany.

The Wynnstay Hunt leaving the Depot, Wrexham, 1950.

Members of the Depot exercising their right, as Freemen, to march through Wrexham with fixed bayonets, 29 March 1952.

'C' Company, 1 RWF, under the Command of Maj. B.G. Pugh, undertaking Internal Security duties in Georgetown, British Guiana, October 1953. The Battalion was stationed in the West Indies from March 1951 to March 1954. During the tour, companies undertook internal security commitments throughout the Caribbean.

Prime Minister Winston Churchill accompanied by Anthony Eden inspects a Guard of Honour in Bermuda in 1953.

Her Majesty The Queen presenting new Colours to the 1st, 2nd and 4th (TA) Battalions at Wroughton Airfield, 23 July 1954.

2 RWF patrol shortly after a successful engagement with Chinese communist terrorists near Gemas, Malaya, 23 April 1956. Back row: Left to right: Fus Evans 66, Cpl Gookin, Cpl Wing. Middle row: Fus Griffiths 74, RSM Meredith, CSM Woods, Fus Jones. Front: L/Cpl Wall.

A draft from the 2nd Battalion en route to the 1st Battalion in Dortmund, Germany, entraining at Lichfield, October 1957.

The Colours of the 2nd Battalion on parade at Wrexham in December 1957, shortly before being disbanded. The Battalion had been reformed in 1952, as part of the expansion of the British Army at the time of the Korean War.

Members of 1 RWF searching for weapons at a check point in Cyprus, 1958/59. The Battalion was involved in operations against EOKA terrorists seeking union with Greece.

Comedian Harry Secombe leading the Drums of 1 RWF during his visit to Cyprus. The Battalion served in Cyprus from May 1958 to December 1959.

The 6th/7th Battalion Cambrian March team, 1961. The Cambrian March was an arduous inter-battalion competition held in Snowdonia. The teams marched from Towyn to Penmaenmawr, and were judged on fieldcraft, navigation, bivouac drill and shooting. The group depicted here includes Capt. J.N. Porter (fourth from left) and Cpl Eddie Parry (extreme right) who, at the age of fifty-four was the team's oldest member.

The Royal Welch Fusiliers take over guard from The Royal Vingt-Deuxième Régiment, their allied regiment of Canada, at La Citadelle, Quebec 1962.

Shenkin, the Regiment's yacht, crewed from time-to-time by all ranks, seen here during the 1960s with Capt. H.M.E. Cadogan at the helm and Cpl Sefton forward.

Lt-Col. R.C.H. Barber MC, commanding officer of 1 RWF, outside his 'basha' (jungle tent), Malaya, early in 1963. The 1st Battalion was sent to Singapore at 24 hours notice in December 1963 in response to the situation in Borneo, where confrontation with Indonesia was in full swing.

The official opening of the Welsh Brigade Depot, Crickhowell, May 1963. The group is led by the three Colonels of the Regiments forming the Welsh Brigade. They are, left to right: Lt-Gen. Sir Charles Coleman (Welch), Gen. Sir Hugh Stockwell (RWF), and Maj.-Gen. Matthews (SWB). They are followed by Col. J.E.T. Willes, Brigade Colonel (RWF), and Lt R.M. Llewellyn (RWF).

Gen. Sir Hugh C. Stockwell GCB, KBE, DSO, Colonel of the Regiment and Deputy Supreme Commander Allied Powers in Europe, inspects the 1st Battalion at Iserlohn, Germany, 1963.

Members of 1 RWF during the battalion's six month tour with the United Nations Peace-Keeping Force In Cyprus (UNFICYP), 1966.

Col. Sgt W. Street, the Pioneer Sergeant, 1 RWF, receiving the British Empire Medal from Major Gen. T. Acton, GOC South-West District, November 1967. The Pioneer Sergeant is the only member of the Regiment allowed to wear a beard.

Gancia Girl, the 45ft trimaran in which Capt. M.J. Minter-Kemp came seventh in the single-handed Trans-Atlantic Race in 1968. His self-steering gear failed early in the voyage, which took thirty days.

Internal Security training in Hong Kong in 1969. The 1st Battalion served in the Colony from 1969 to 1971.

Border Patrol in Hong Kong, November 1969. Corporal Rowlands of the 1st Battalion sending a report on his A41 radio.

A 'lion dance' at the opening of a new village in Hong Kong in 1971, being watched by Fus. Landrygan, Lt-Col. C. Hince (commanding officer), Fus. Harvey and Capt. D. Goodchild.

Uniforms worn by the 1st Battalion in Hong Kong, October 1970. As part of the Welsh Brigade (1960-70) the Regiment wore the Brigade cap badge of Prince of Wales's Feathers, although retaining the 'RWF' shoulder title and white hackle in certain orders of dress.

'No Tea for Taffs': Royal Welch Fusiliers on patrol in Fountain Street, Strabane, 1973. When trouble resurfaced in Ireland in 1969, the British Army was initially welcomed by the Republican community and soldiers were often offered tea by the residents of catholic estates. By 1973 attitudes had changed completely, as this photograph of republican graffiti (written for the benefit of 1 RWF) illustrates.

1 RWF in action on the streets of Londonderry, 1972. Note the riot shields, face visors and riot guns designed to fire plastic bullets.

The Royal Welch receiving the Freedom of Cardiff, 7 November 1973. The Regiment has been honoured with the 'Freedom' of many Welsh towns including Wrexham, Caernarfon, Flint, Conwy, Merthyr Tydfil, Swansea and Colwyn Bay.

Vehicle Check Point (VCP), Strabane, 1973, known to soldiers as 'The Hump', manned by members of 1 RWF.

Presentation of Colours to the 1st and 3rd (V) Battalions by Her Majesty The Queen at Caernarfon Castle, 7 November 1975.

Members of 1 RWF uncovering an IRA arms cache, Northern Ireland, 1979.

Chelsea Pensioners CSM Briggs and Sgt Barber (Royal Welch veterans of the 1st and 2nd World Wars respectively) visiting the Regimental Museum at Caernarfon Castle in 1980. The first museum curator, Maj. E.L. Kirby MC, TD, DL, accompanies them.

Men of 3 RWF in training with soldiers of the Arkansas National Guard, USA 1981. WO2 Jarvis ('HQ' Coy) is standing at the rear of the group with Sgt Colin Roberts ('A' Coy) kneeling in the foreground.

1 RWF on exercise in Germany, 1981. Col.-Sgt Alun Davies mans the gun of an FV 432 Armoured Personnel Carrier, during mechanized vehicle training.

HM The Queen, Colonel-in-Chief, being assisted in cutting the Tercentenary cake by the Colonel of the Regiment, Brigadier A.C. Vivian, at Powis Castle on 21 April 1989.

Members of the 6th Cadet Battalion, RWF, on exercise. The RWF currently has two cadet battalions, the 4th and 6th based at Kinmel Park and Bethesda (North Wales) respectively.

'Fear that the RWF will merge with the Cheshire Regiment', cartoon by Holland Roberts published in the *Daily Post*, 15 July 1991. Defence cuts in the early 1990s threatened to end the 300-year history of the RWF by amalgamating it with the Cheshire Regiment. However, a well-organised and vigorous campaign to 'Save the Fusiliers' had the desired effect, and both regiments were reprieved.

Territorial soldiers of 3 RWF during training manoeuvres in Scotland, 1994. In 1999 the battalion was amalgamated with the 2nd Battalion Royal Regiment of Wales to form a single Welsh TA unit, the Royal Welsh Regiment.

Men of the 1st Battalion manning Observation Post Two, overlooking Gorazde, Bosnia 1995. The RWF was sent to Bosnia in 1995 as part of the United Nation Protection Force (UNPROFOR). During the tour thirt-three member of the battalion were taken hostage by the Bosnian Serbs. They were later released unharmed.

Lt-Col. J.P. Riley, commanding officer of 1 RWF in Bosnia, 1995. Col. Riley was awarded the Distinguished Service Order (DSO) for the tour in Bosnia. On his right arm he wears the United Nation brassard with embroidered regimental title.

Gorazde Camp under fire, Bosnia 1995. A mortar round explodes just outside the camp, observed by a fusilier from his Armoured Personnel Carrier (APC).

Recipients of awards for the UN Tour in Bosnia (1995) at Buckingham Palace 12 May 1996. Left to right: Maj. R.J. Westley MC, Lt H.N.C. Nightingale MC, Sgt D.H. Parry MC, Col. J.P. Riley DSO, Col.-Sgt P. Humphreys CGC, WO2 A. Jaques MBE, WO2 M.J. Jones 57 MBE.

Fusilier Ricky Nicholson, World and
Commonwealth Kickboxing Champion
with his Commonwealth title belt, 1996.

The RWF of America marching in La Citadelle, Quebec, behind the Regimental Goat of the
Royal Vingt-Deuxième Régiment. This American re-enactment group is dedicated to the
accurate portrayal of the RWF during the War of Independence (1775-83). They have taken
part in several regimental pageants, including the tercentenary celebrations in 1989.

Her Majesty The Queen presenting new Colours to the 1st Battalion at Beachley Barracks, Chepstow, in May 1996. The Queen is assisted by the Senior Major, P.A. Robson, and attended by the Colonel of the Regiment, Maj.-Gen. R.M. Llewellyn CB, OBE. Ensigns to the Colours are 2nd-Lt Clayton and 2nd-Lt Hackney.

1 RWF rugby team after winning the Army Rugby Union Challenge Cup, 2000. This was the first time the RWF had won the competition, and the first time the trophy has gone to an infantry battalion since 1986.